$3,00

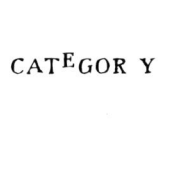

CAT^EGOR Y

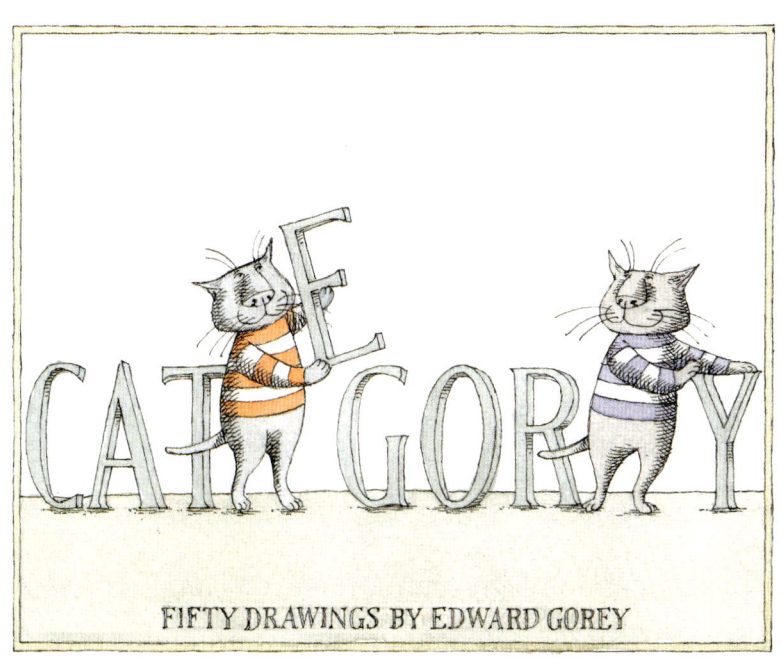

CATEGORY

FIFTY DRAWINGS BY EDWARD GOREY

Pomegranate

SAN FRANCISCO

Published by Pomegranate Communications, Inc.
Box 808022, Petaluma CA 94975
800 227 1428; www.pomegranate.com

Pomegranate Europe Ltd.
Unit 1, Heathcote Business Centre, Hurlbutt Road
Warwick, Warwickshire CV34 6TD, UK
[+44] 0 1926 430111; sales@pomeurope.co.uk

Pomegranate Catalog No. A125
Printed in China
14 13 12 11 10 09 08 07 06   10 9 8 7 6 5 4 3 2 1

For Miss Edna

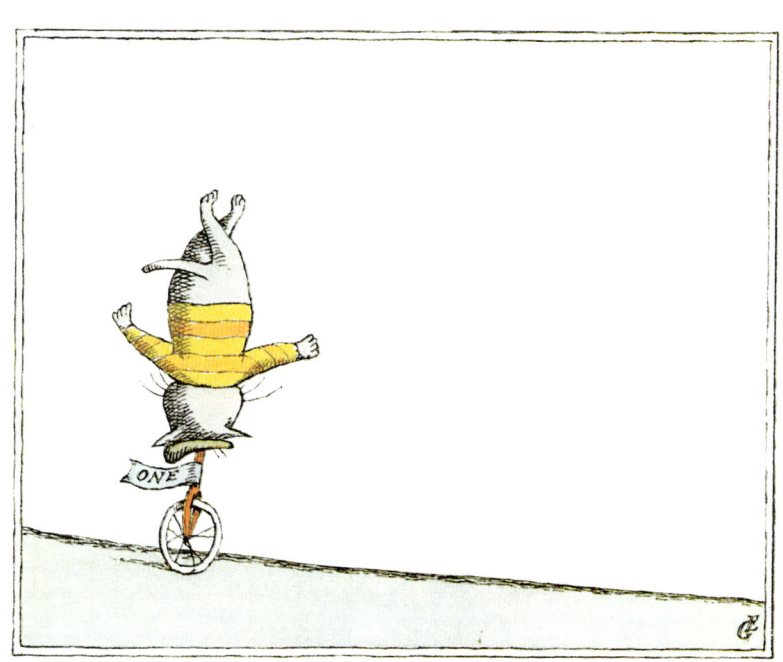

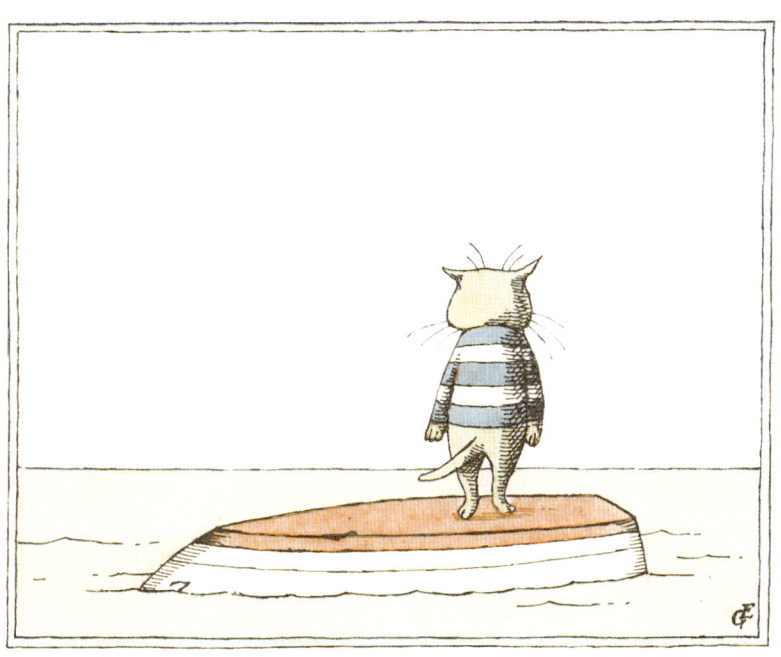

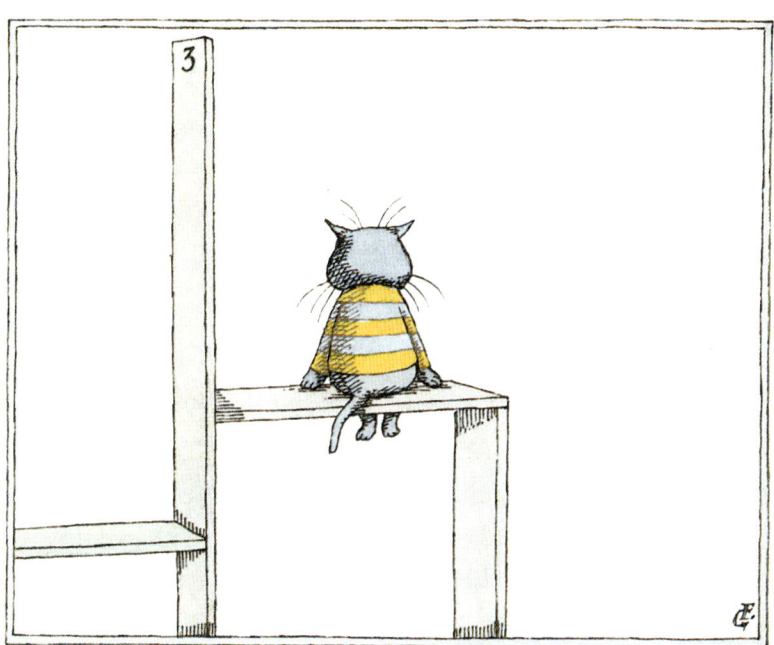

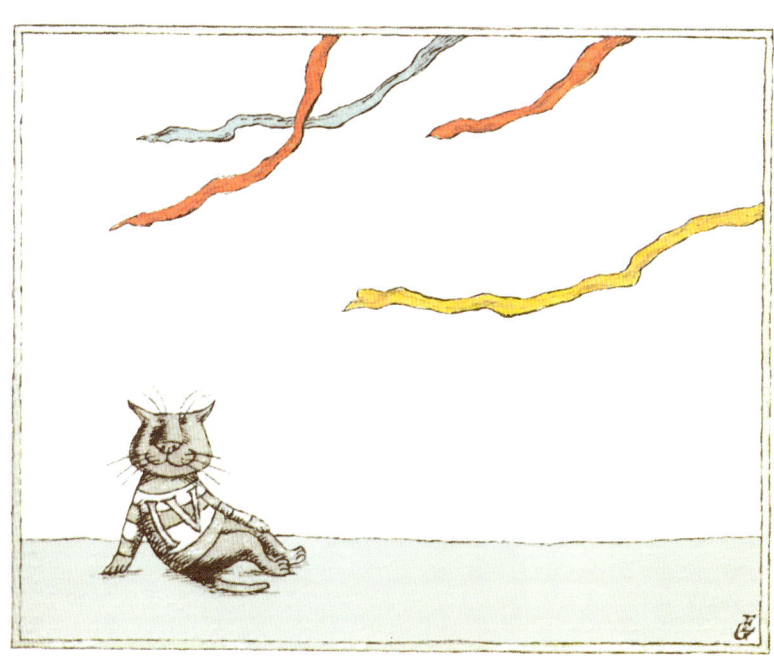

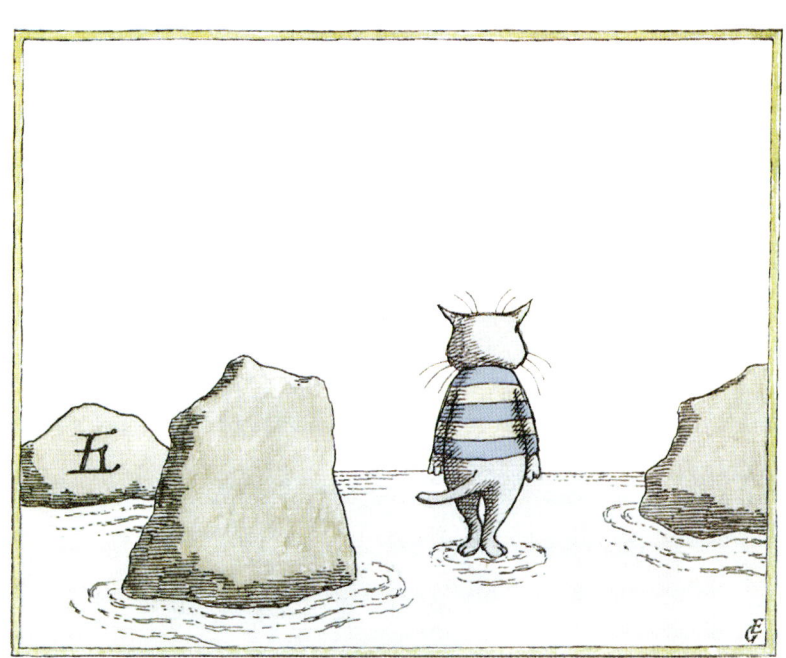

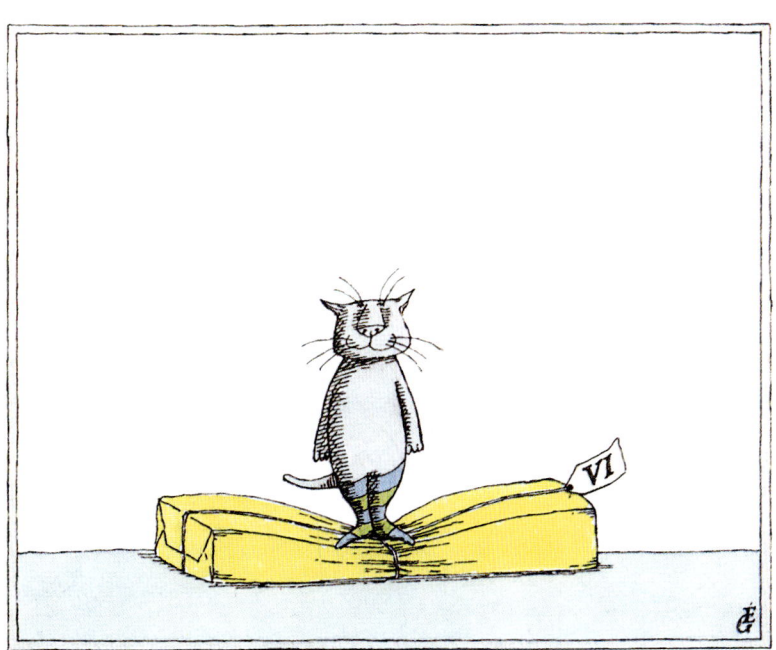

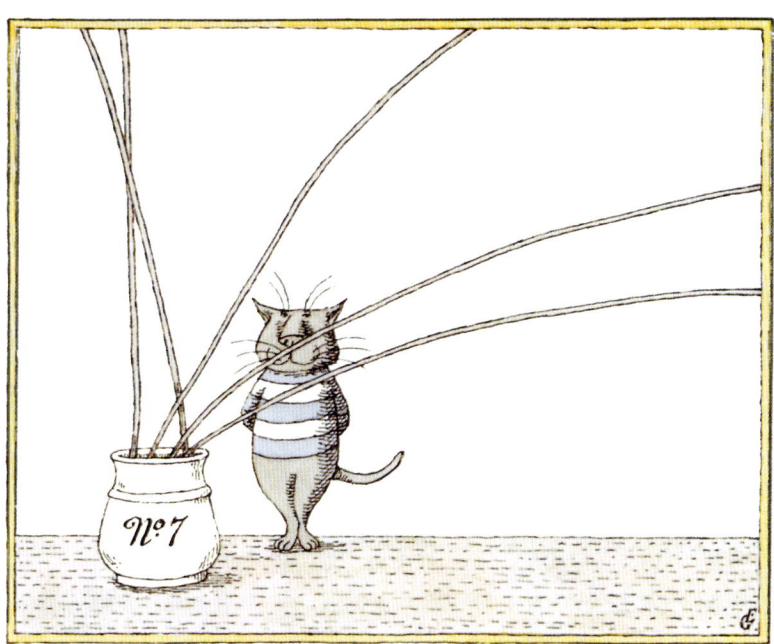

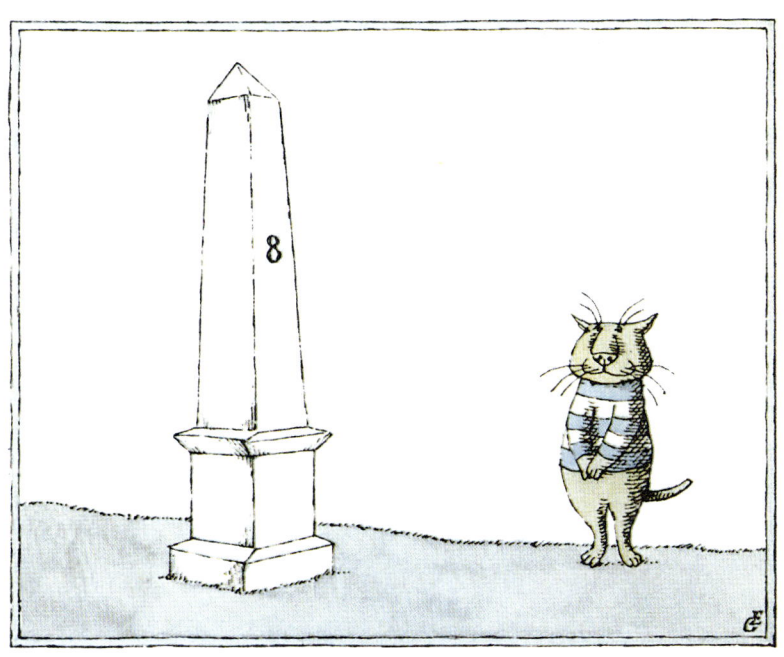

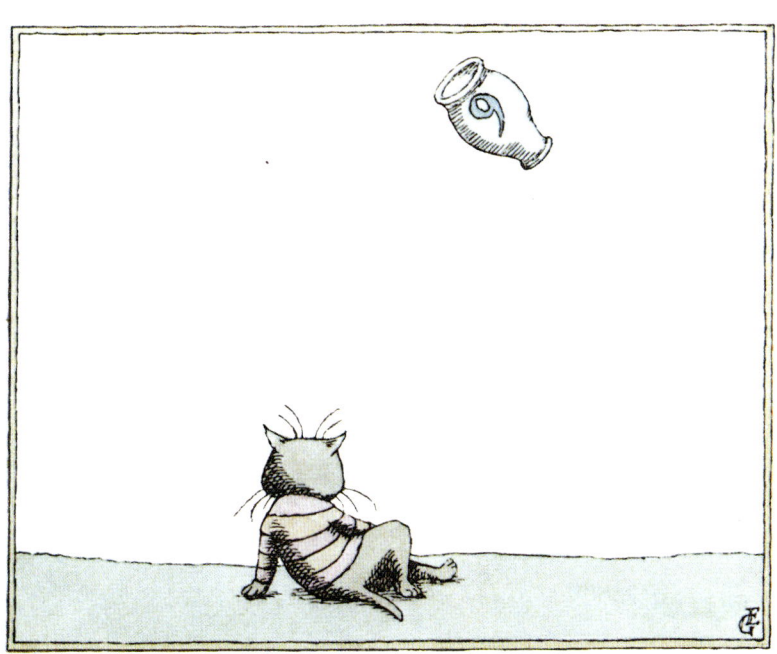

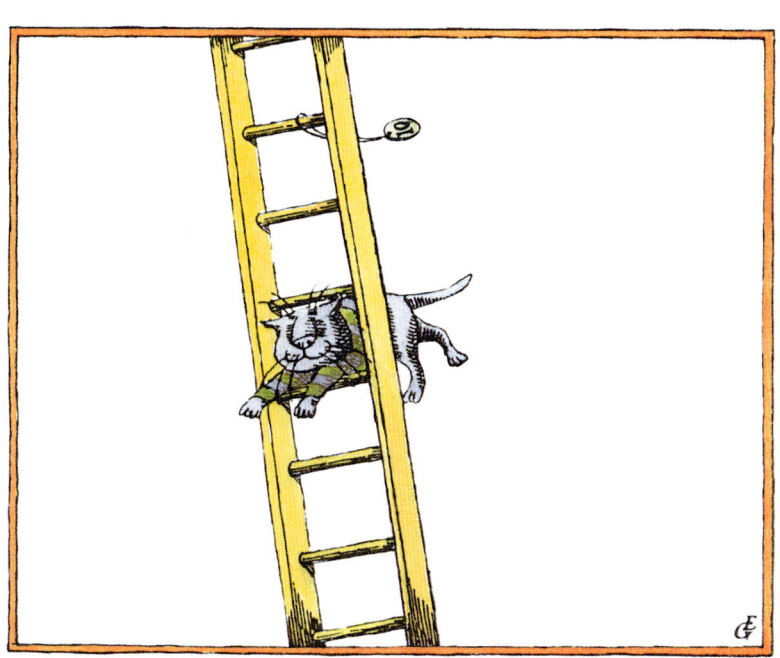

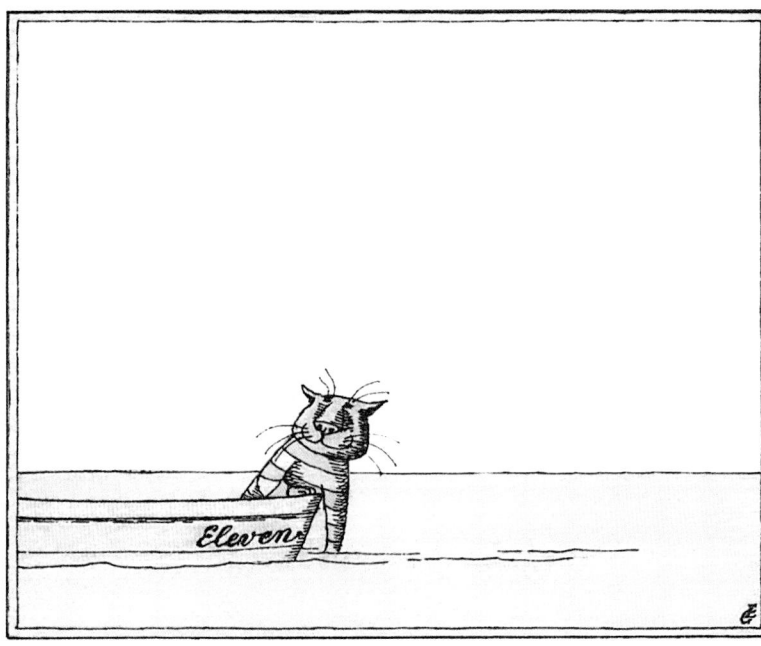

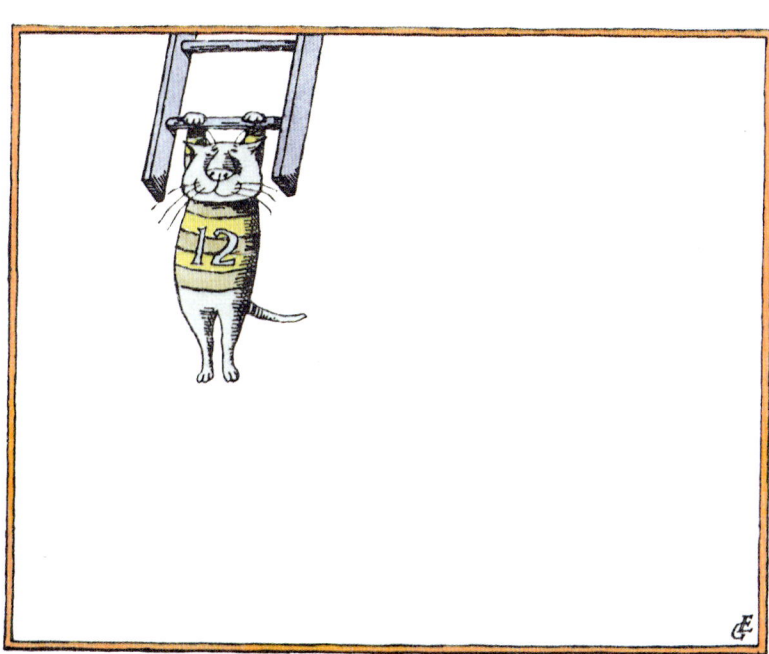

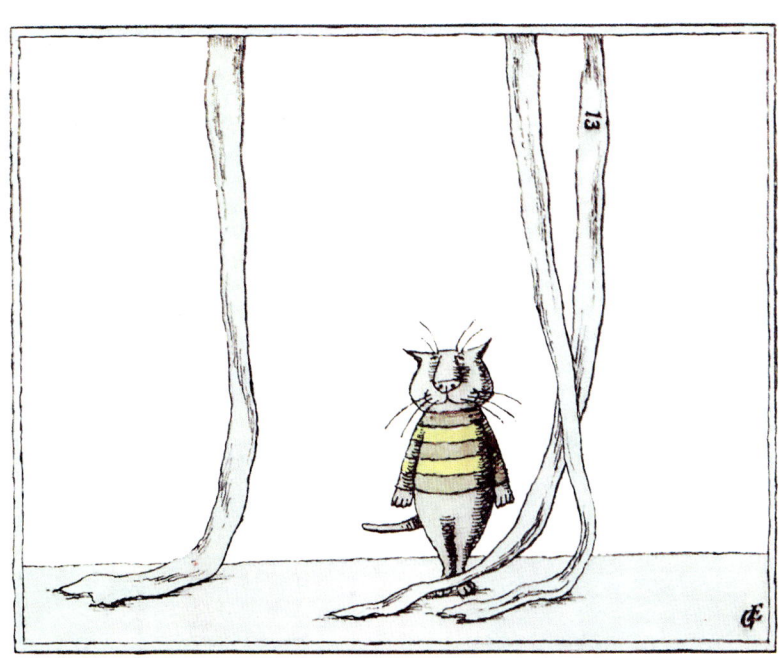

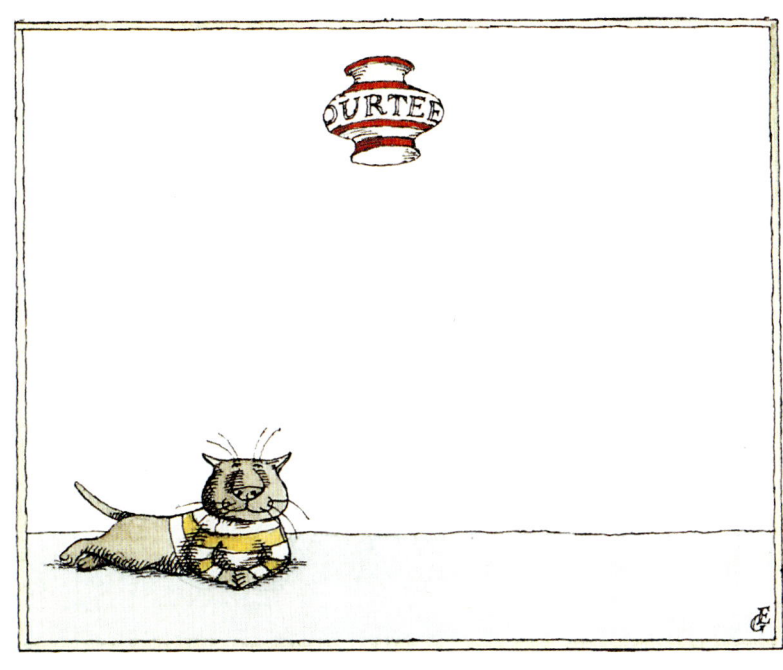

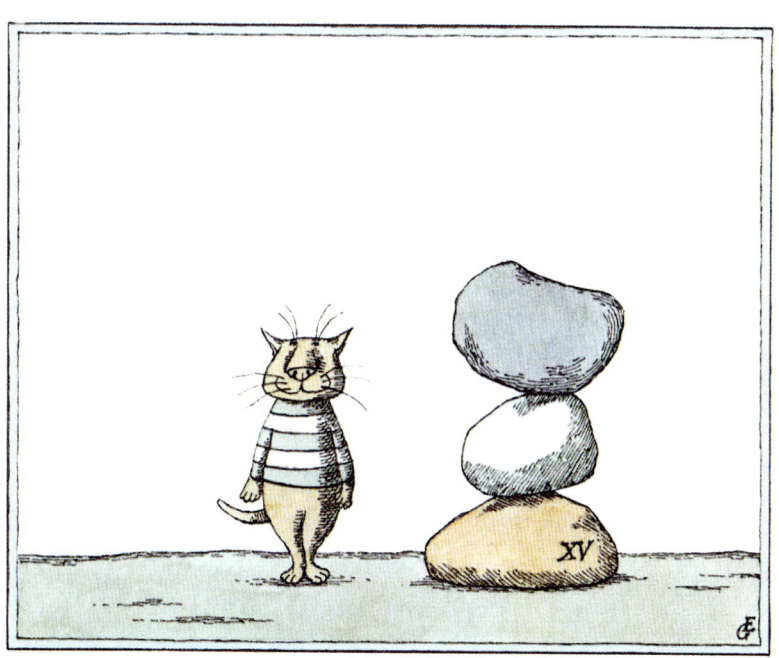

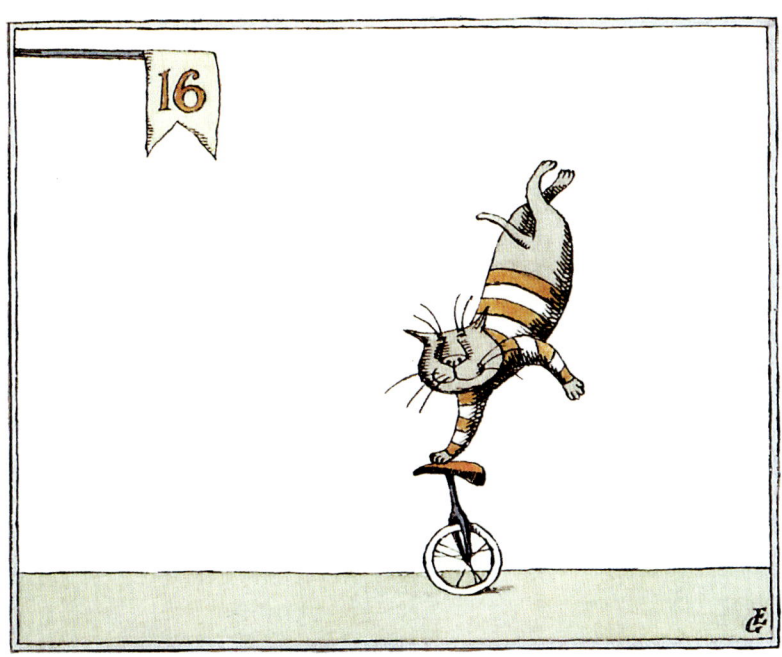

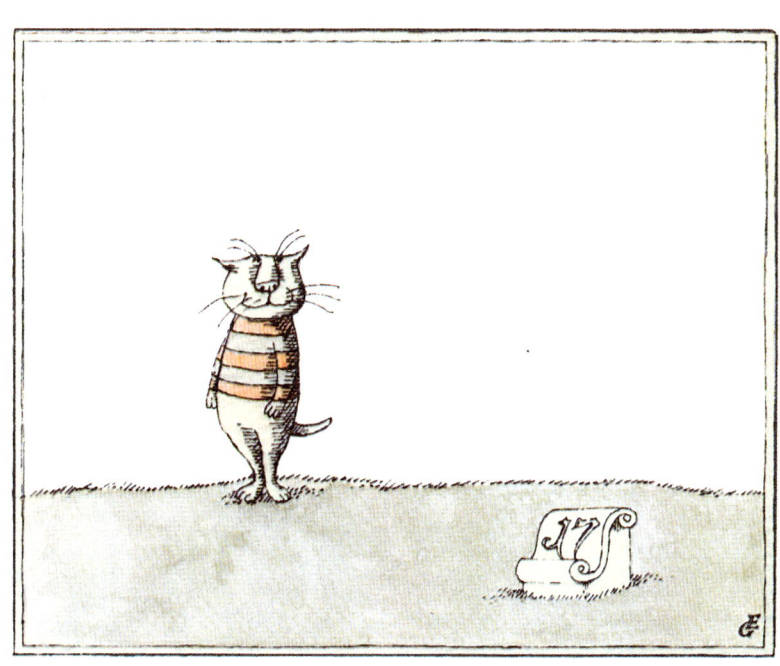

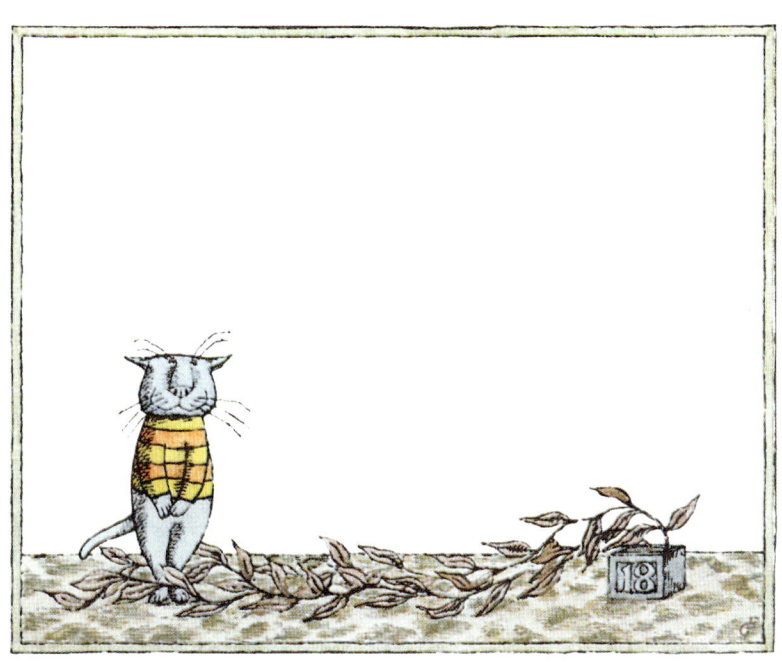

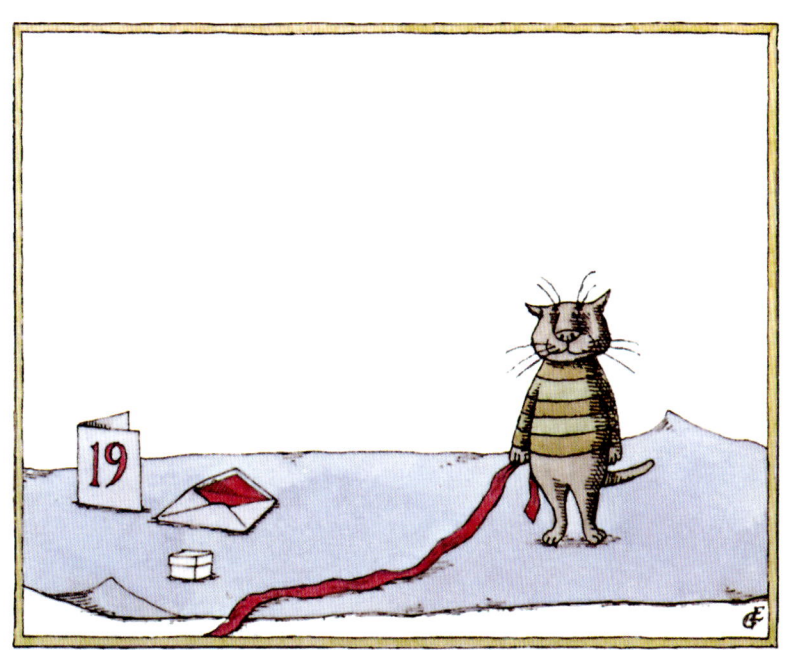

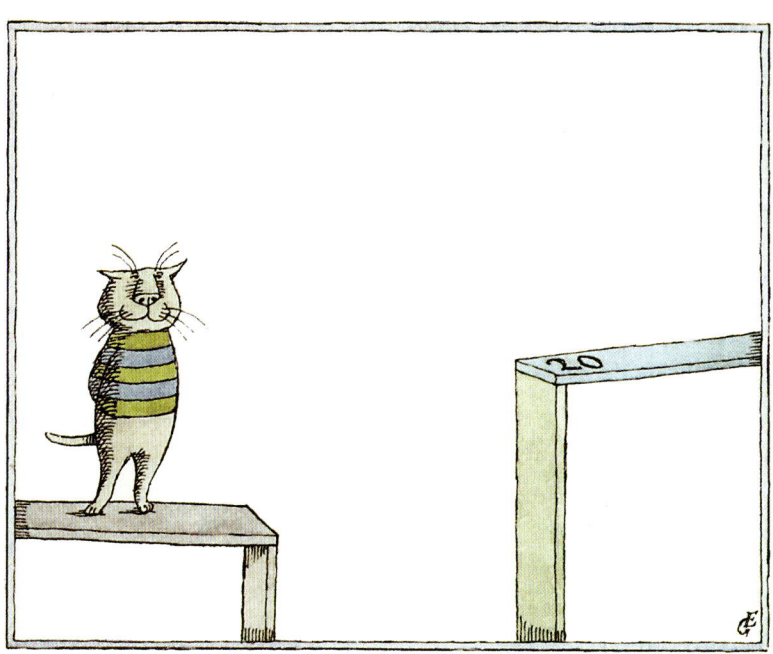

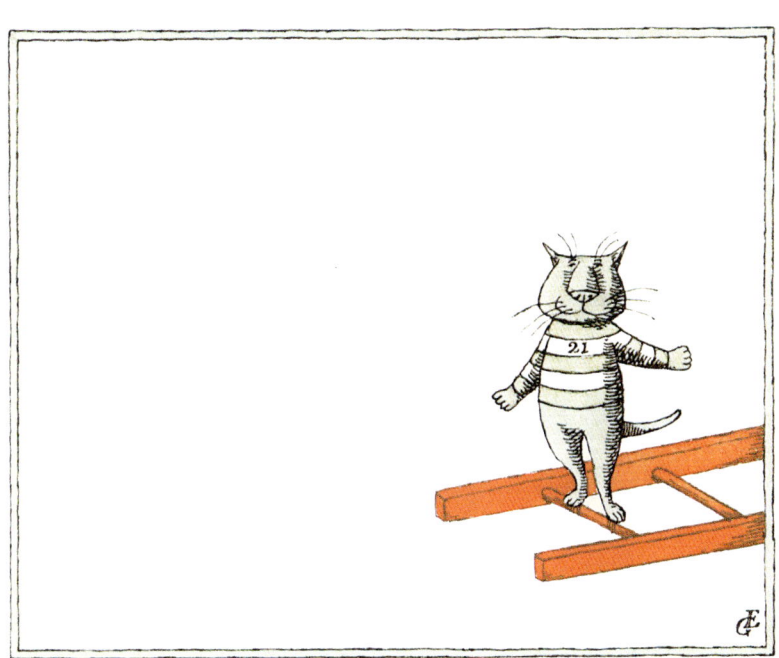

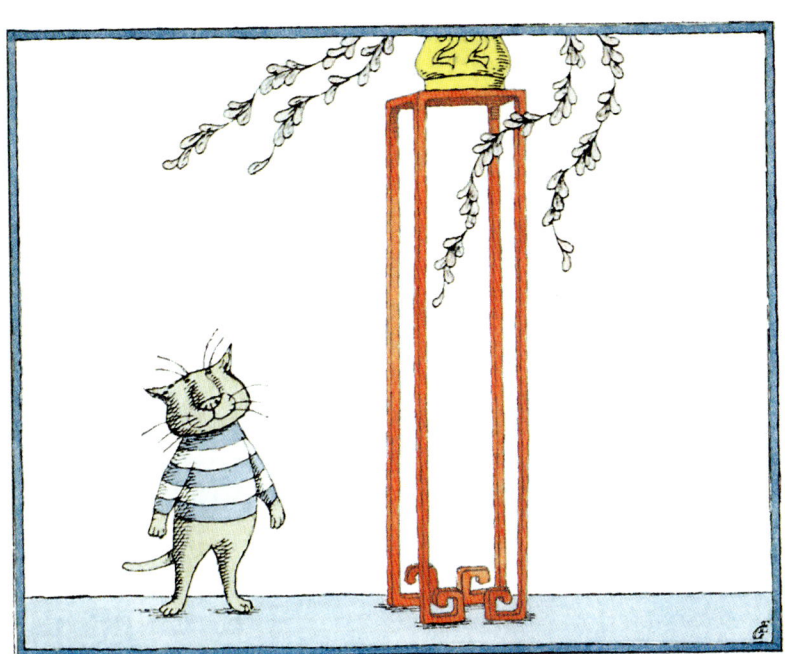

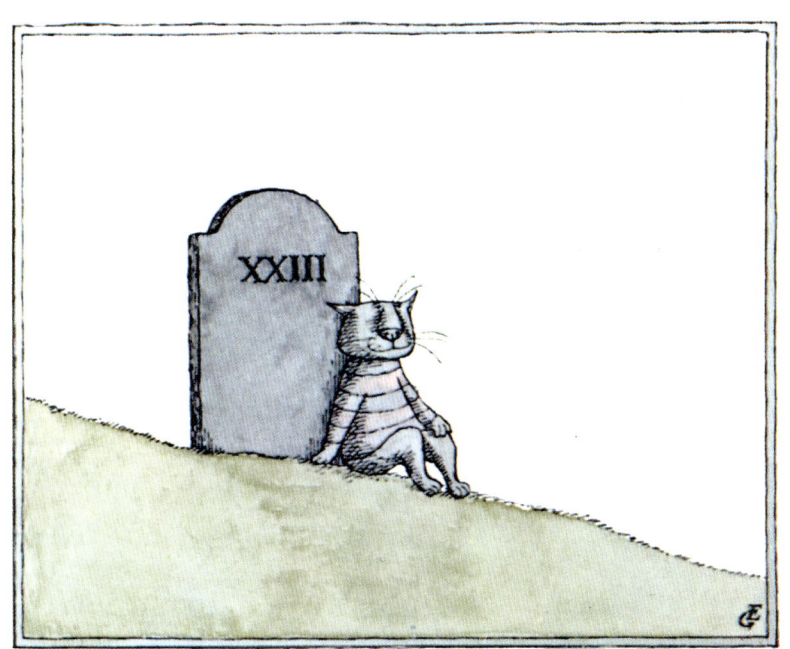

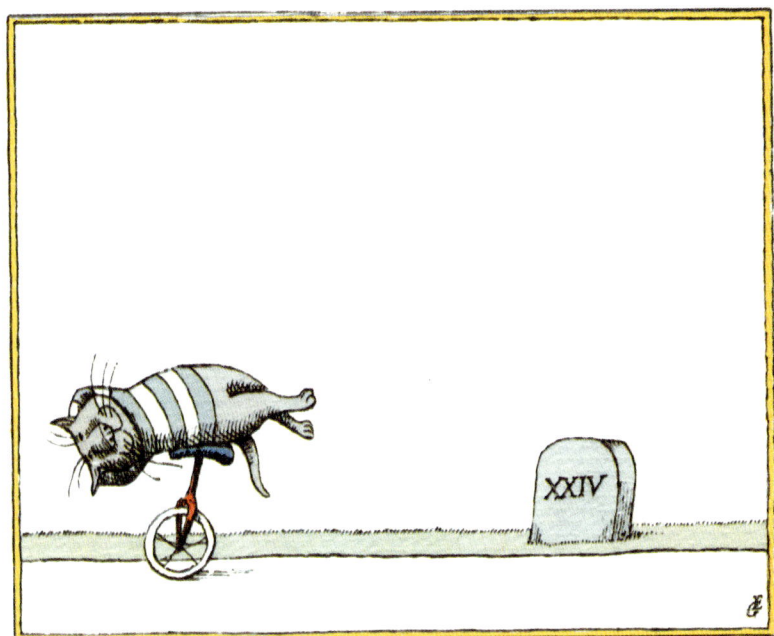

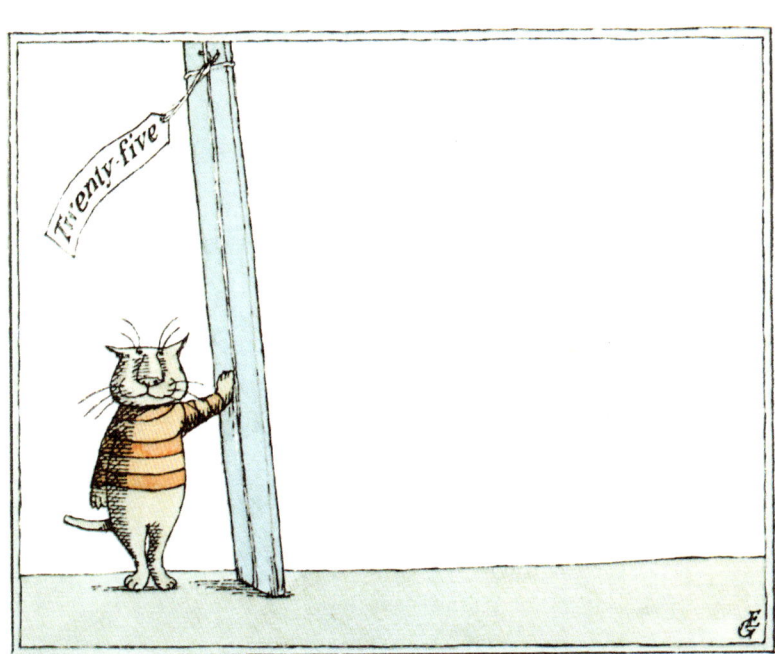

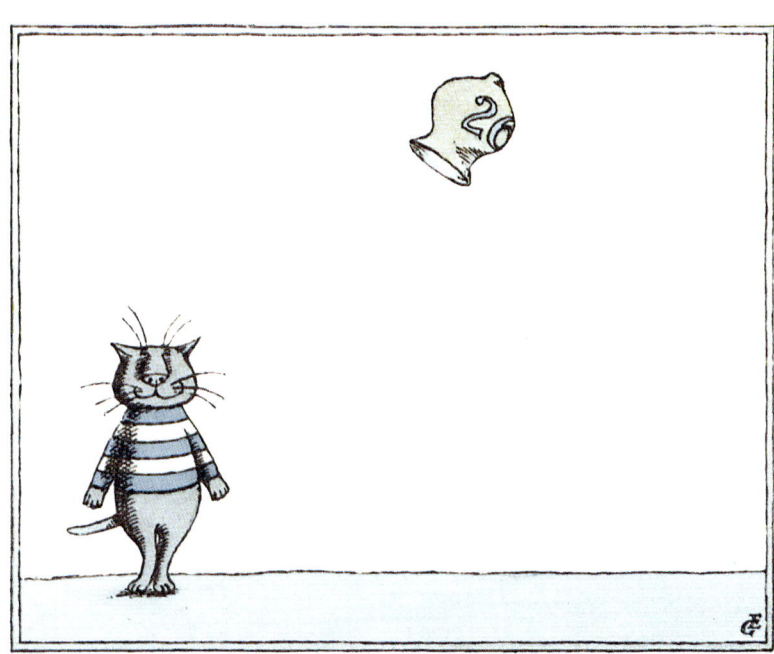

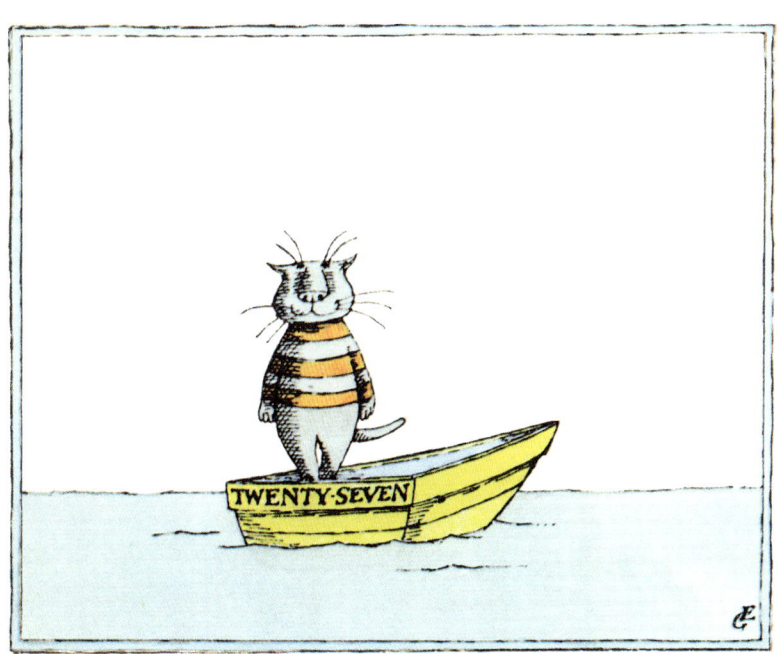

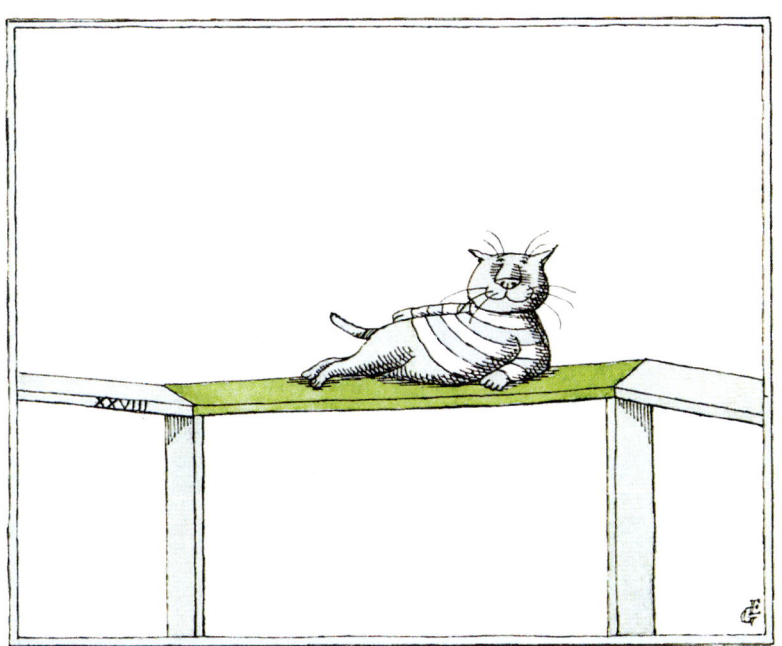

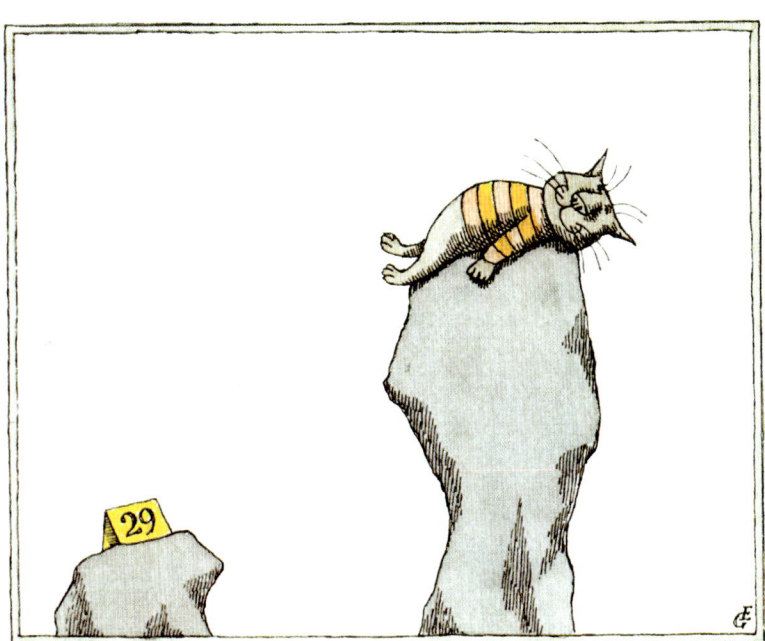

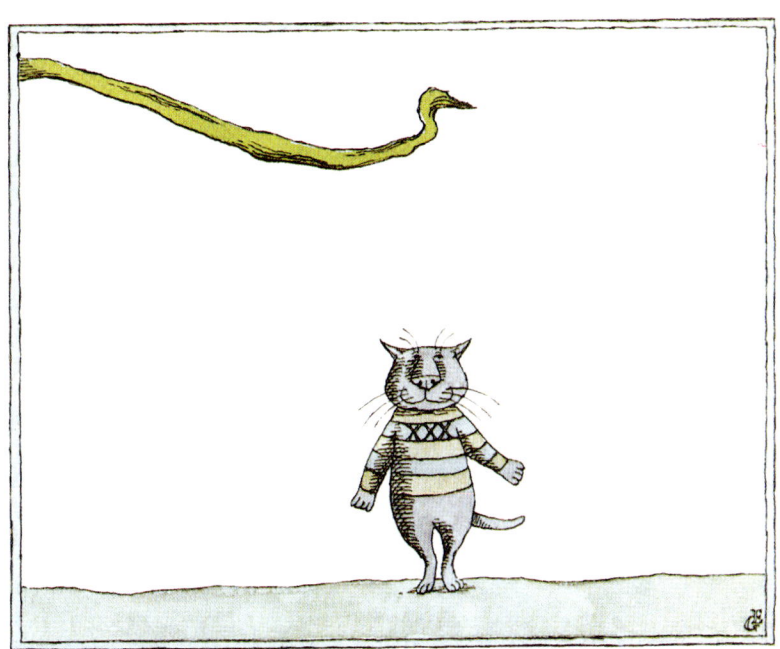

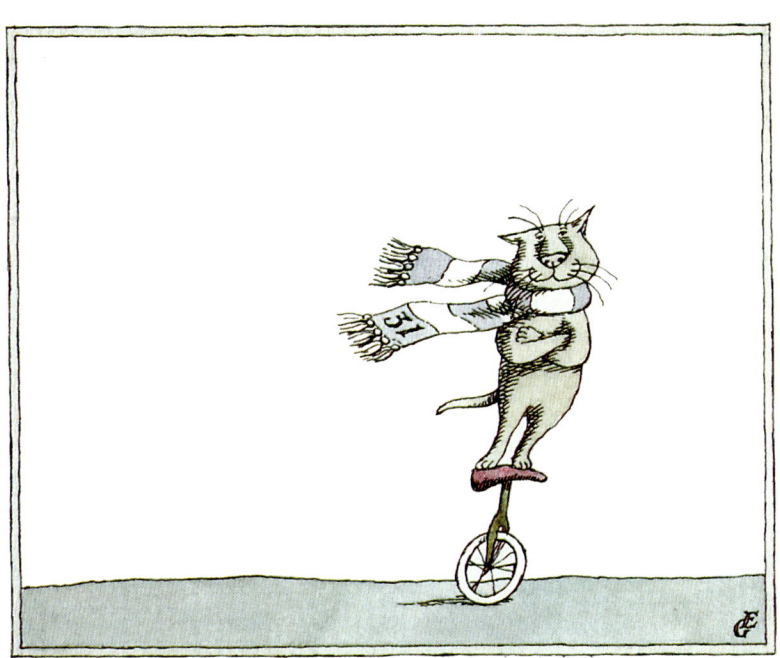

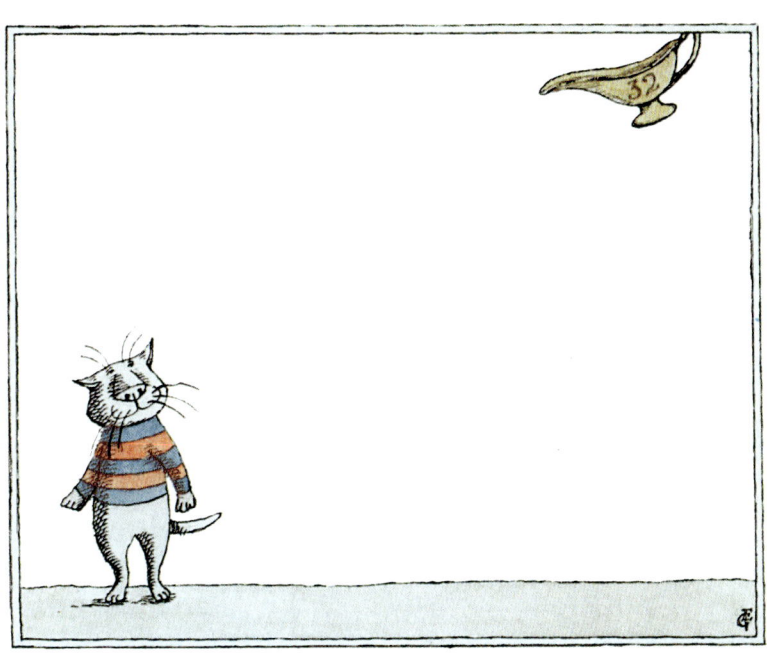

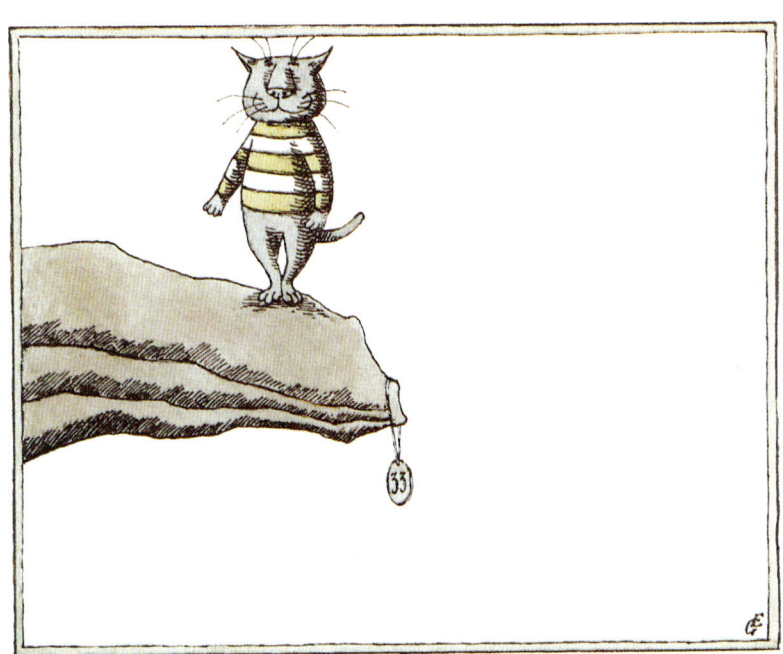

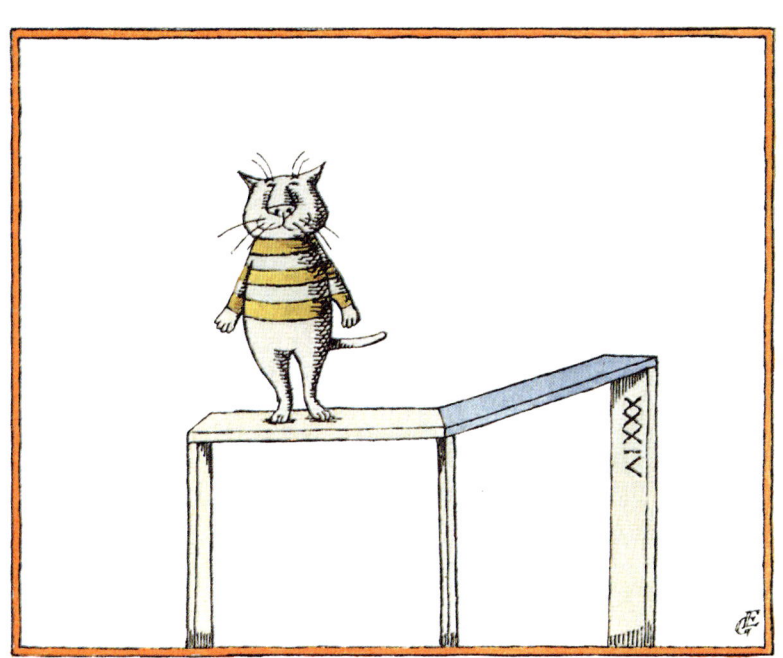

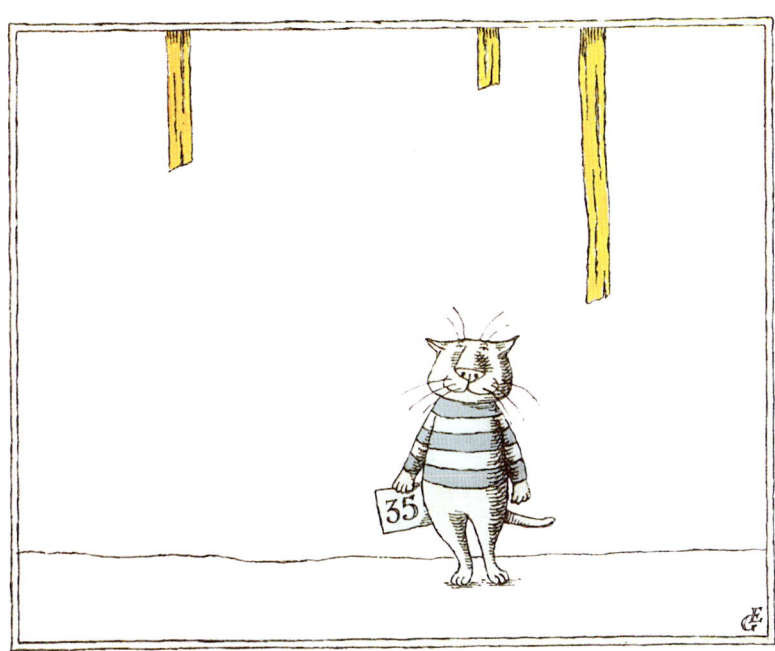

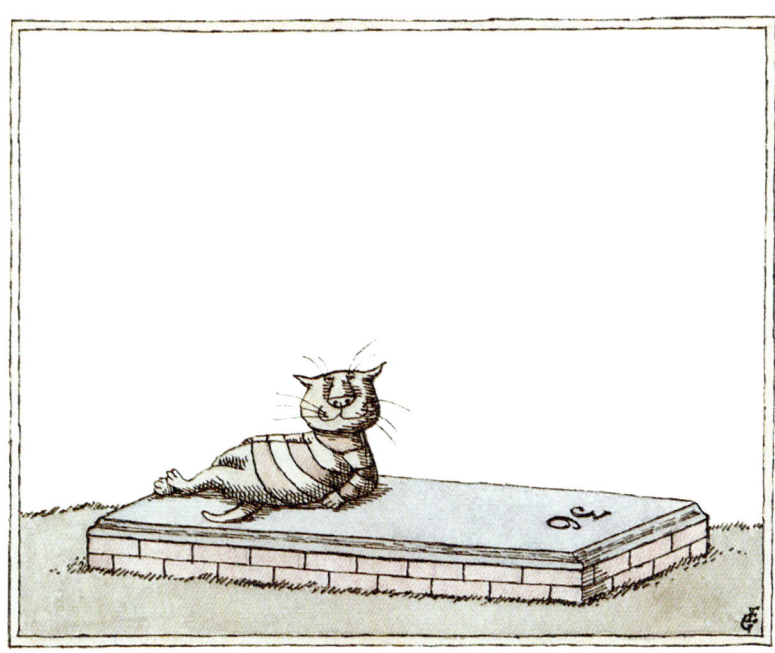

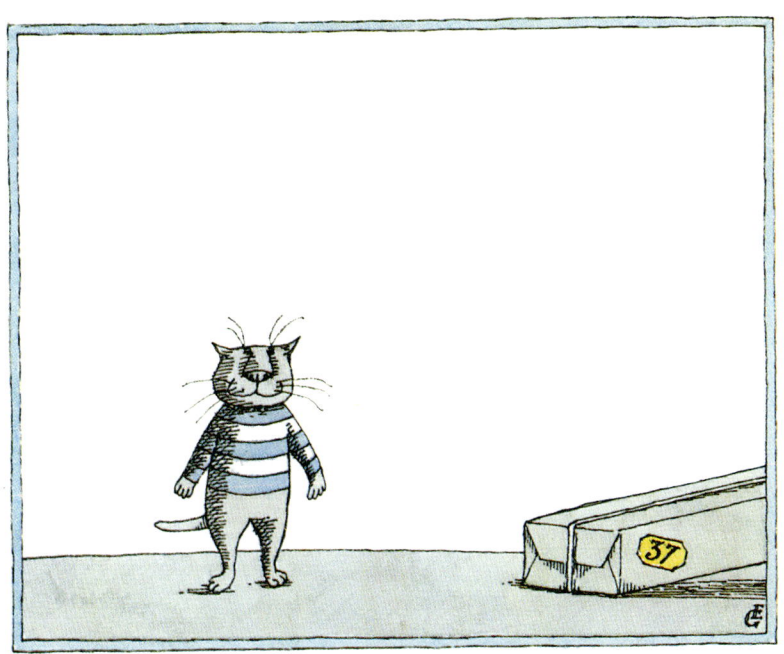

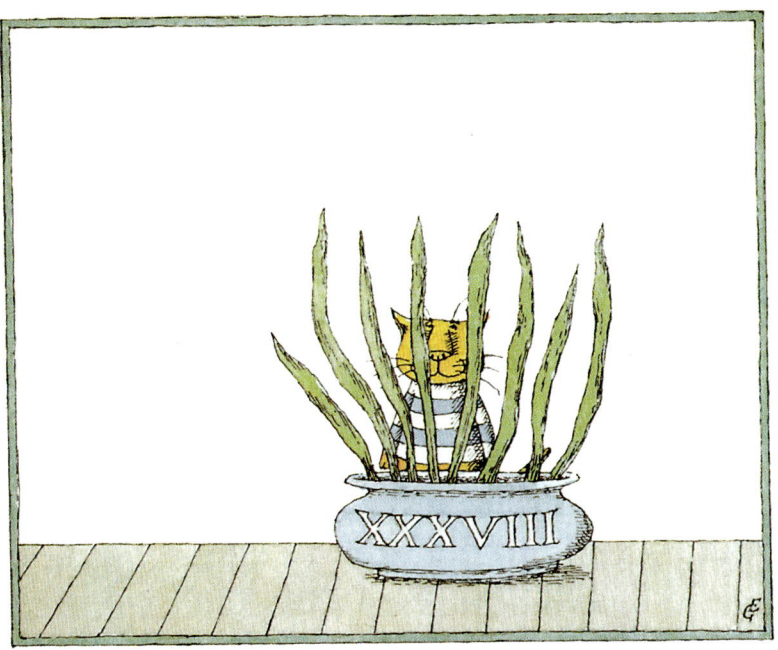

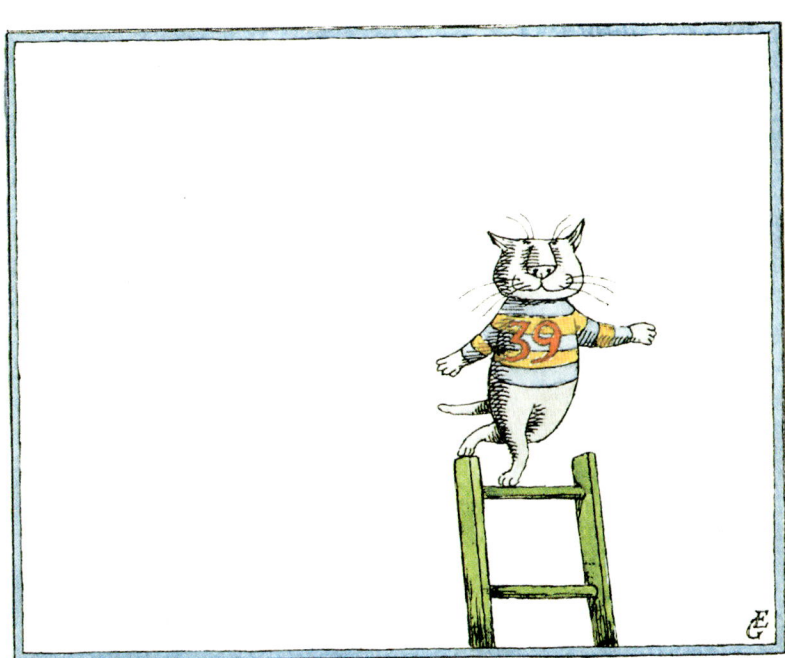

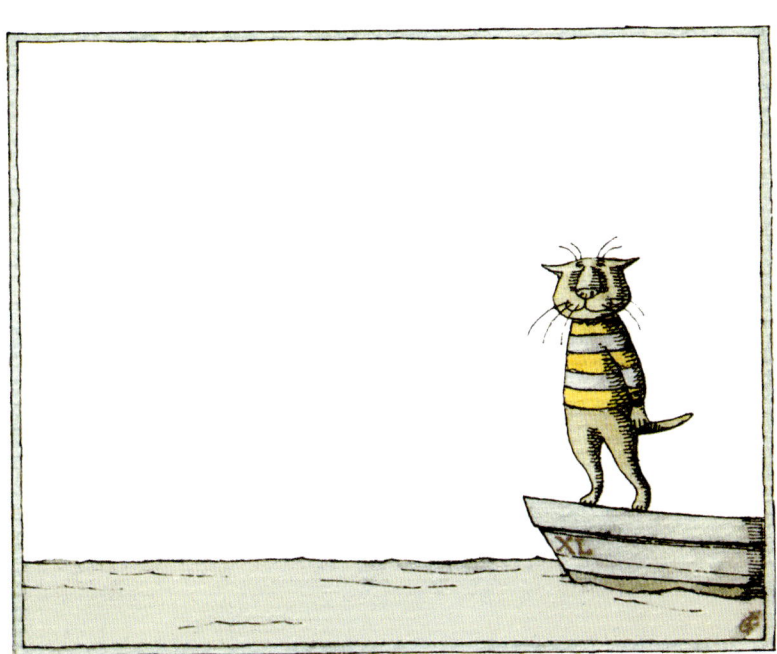

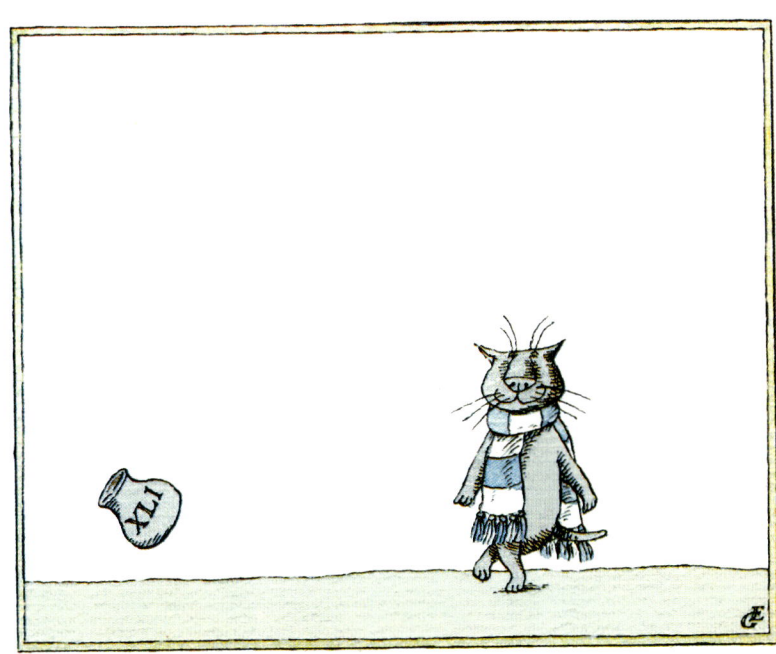

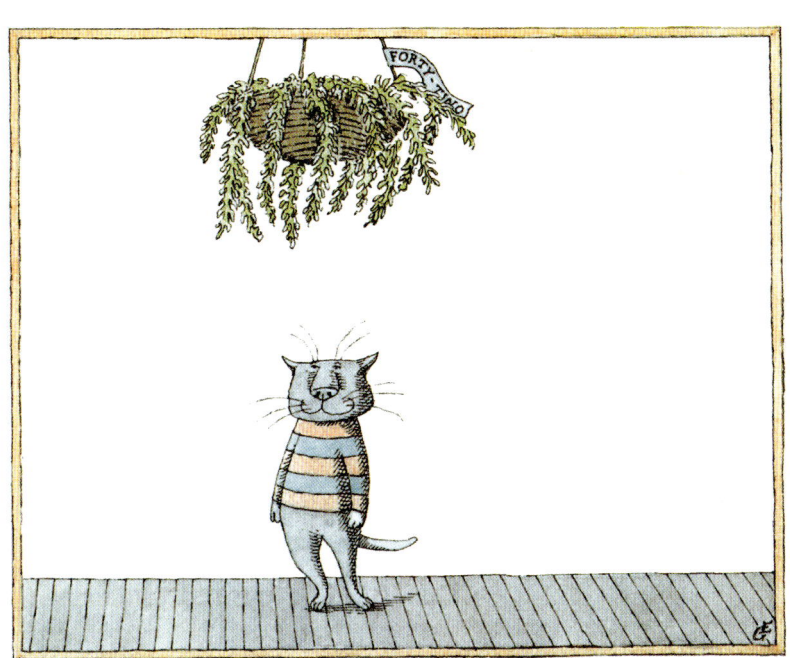

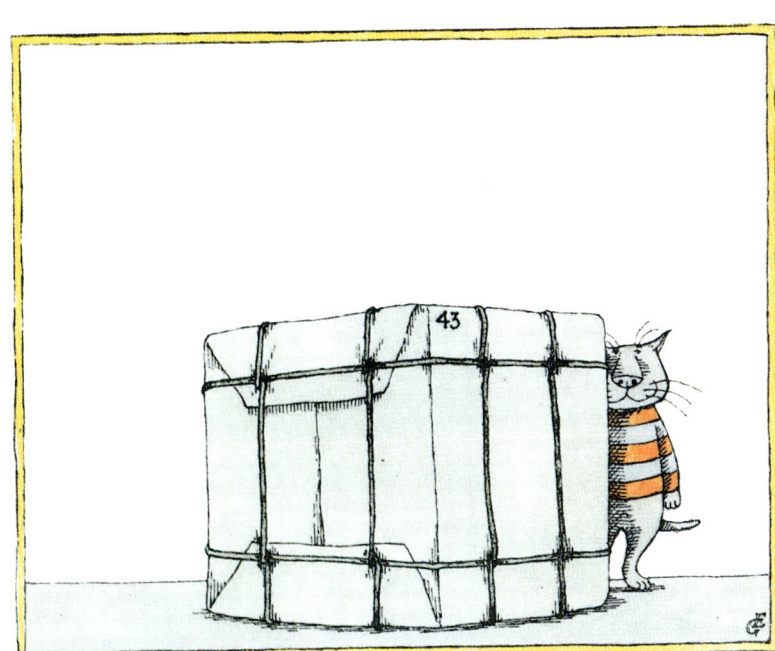

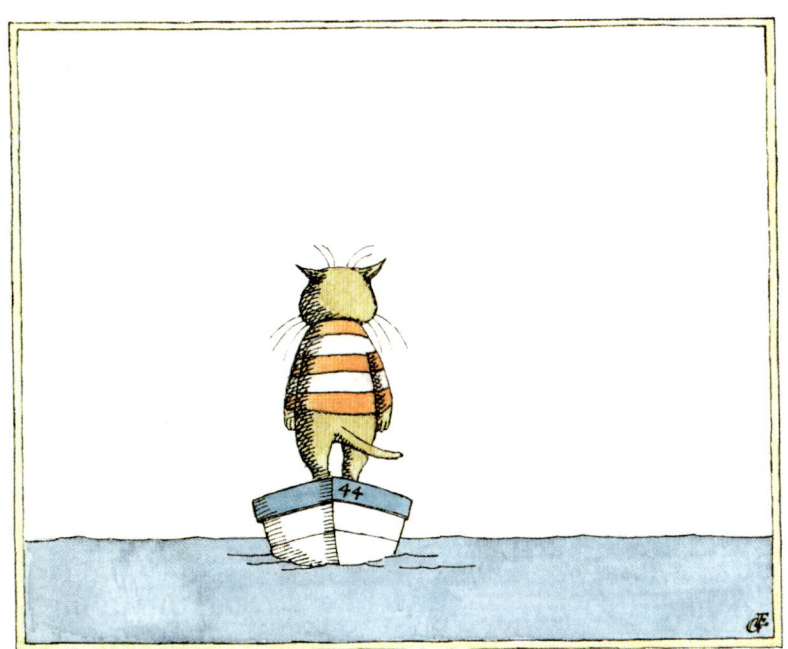

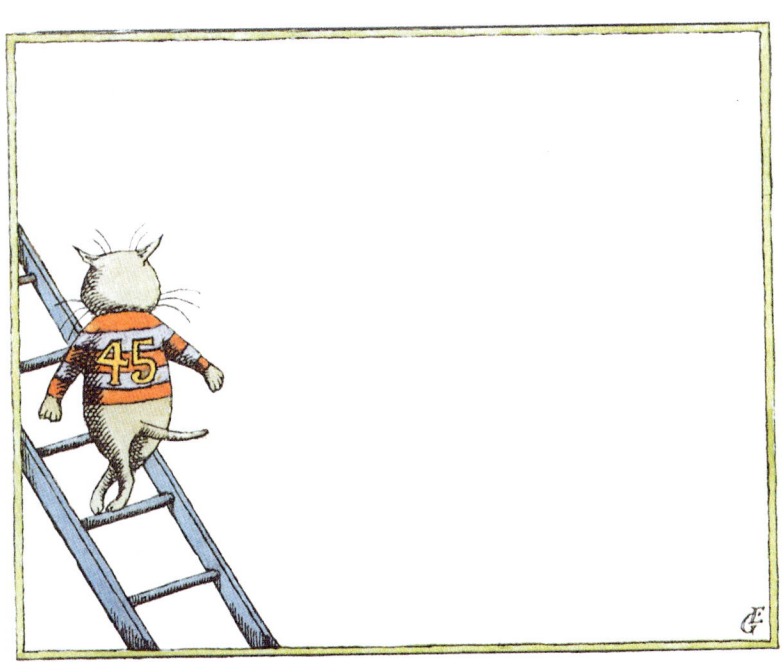

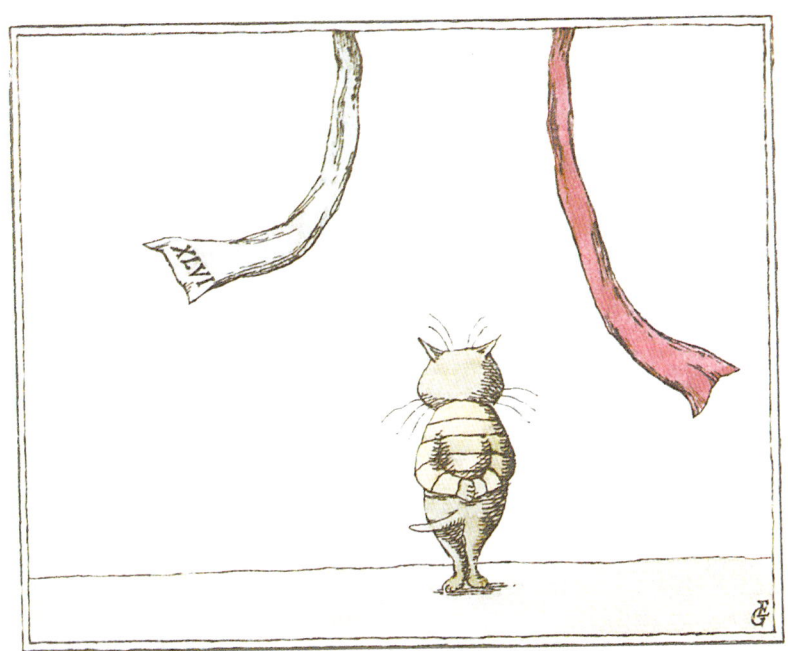

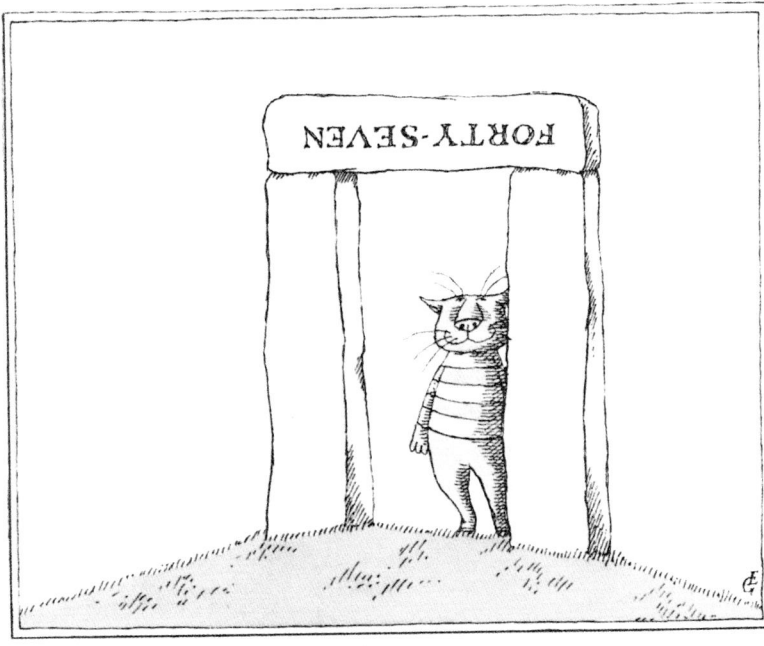

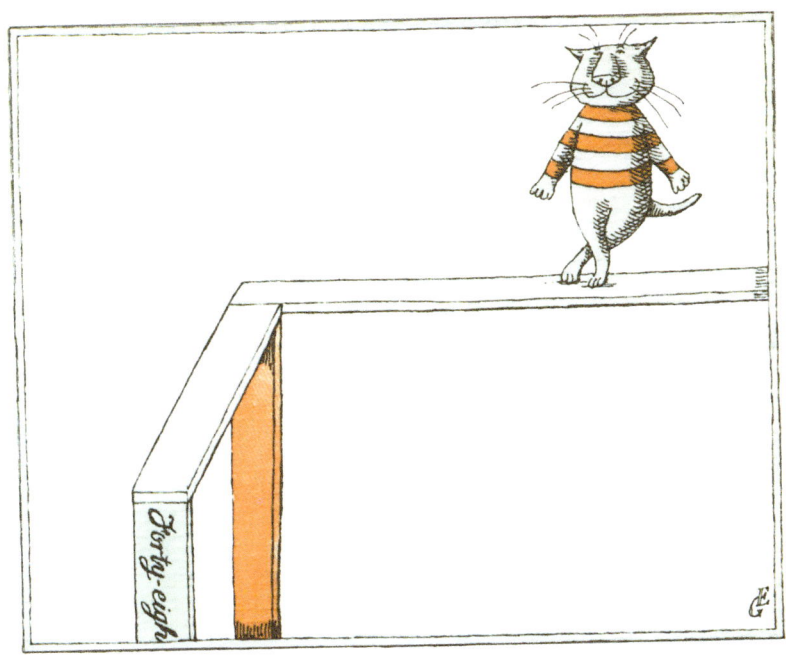

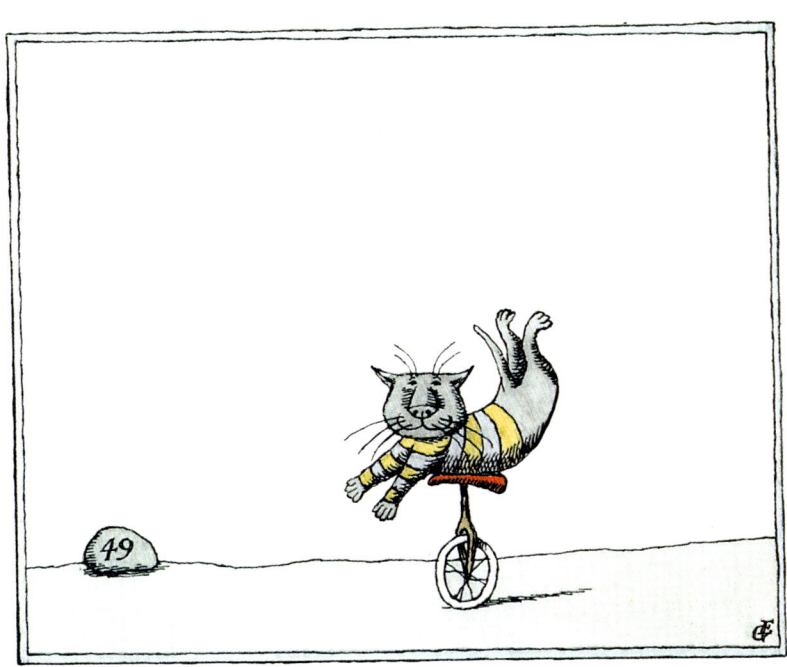

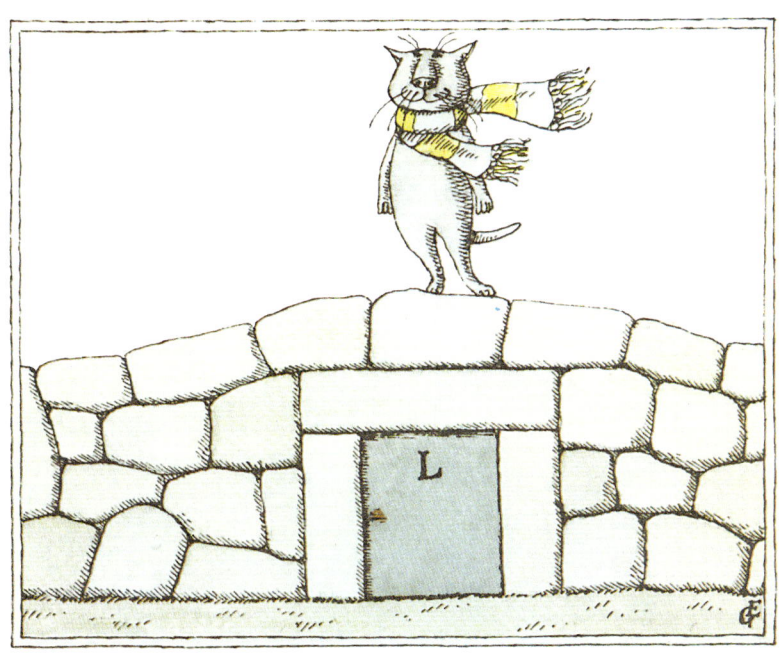

The originals of these drawings
were done to accompany the
limited edition of *Amphigorey.*

The first edition of CAT^EGOR Y
was published May 1973 in
wrappers, with a limited edition
of 100 numbered copies signed
by the artist, in special binding,
and slipcased.